CHAPTER ONE

Introduction

On Friday, March 24th, 2017, I finished an afternoon workout with my friends at the local gym. After training, my friend John mentioned to me that cold showers were a great way to relieve sore muscles after a grueling workout, and that I should take one when I got home. I was very skeptical of my friend, after all, who would want to take a freezing cold shower?! The mere thought of stepping under a stream of ice cold water made me start to shiver. Despite my skepticism, I decided I would take on my friends challenge. If he could do it, why wouldn't I be able to as well I thought to myself. When I got home that afternoon, I took my first freezing cold shower. I turned the tap in my shower down as cold as it could go, and I walked in. As the ice cold stream of water flowed down on my body, I naturally gasped for air and began to breathe heavily. Innately, my body was trying to get in as much oxygen as possible to keep myself warm. This state of semi-shock (a result of my body adjusting to the frigid temperature) lasted about 30 or so seconds until I started to feel better adjusted. I stayed in the shower for a total of 3 minutes that afternoon. As I dried myself off, my body started to warm rapidly from the increased blood flow circulation I was experiencing. I felt invigorated, I was alert, and my muscles even felt a little less sore. Put simply, I felt transformed. I remember thinking to myself, how could such a simple activity rapidly yield such great, observable results? I knew that I was on to something. After my first cold shower experience, I knew I should continue to have cold showers be a part of my life routine. I conducted additional research on the subject of cold showers, and I was excited for my next one. I went on to have cold showers for a month straight that Spring. The cold shower became a daily ritual of mine, and one I enjoyed most mornings and evenings. Not only was I gaining vast physical and mental benefits through this routine, but I was also challenging myself on a daily basis. The cold shower became a trial I willingly faced day after day. This willingness to face the obstacle of a cold shower is a key benefit and will be discussed in detail later. When I discuss my habit of taking a cold shower with friends and relatives, I often hear the same thing over and over. The conversation goes something like this...

Friend: "What do you do to help with muscle fatigue or soreness."

Me: "I actually take a lot of cold showers for about 3-5 minutes. I find they help relieve soreness in my muscles and joints, and there is a wealth of research to back this up. They also help me with my mood and focus. Cold showers are pretty awesome, you should try one sometime!"

Friend: "Wow- that's pretty cool. I do cold showers too, but I usually start the shower hot and then go to cold water at the end for 20 seconds."

Me: "Nice. You should try to do a full shower start to finish cold though."

Friend: "Yeah I'm not sure, that might be too cold for me..."

A lot of people expose themselves to cold water in the shower as was the case with my friend in the example above, but very few actually do full cold showers from start to finish. Taking a regular shower and ending it cold is known as an "Irish shower". I highly advise that you reject the Irish shower method of "easing your way into a cold shower" by starting warm and finishing cold. If you are serious and committed to experiencing the physical and mental benefits of cold showers- you need to attack the challenge head on and go straight into cold water right away. There is no way around this. So do not deviate from this rule- keep the water cold the whole way through! This is the only way you will condition your mind and body to handle the cold showers properly and reap the full benefits of them. Trust me, when you get through your first handful of cold showers you will feel great. You will also feel proud that you challenged yourself in this way.

CHAPTER TWO

Taking Your First Cold Shower

For your first cold shower, I advise you to prepare with 45 seconds of deep breathing to maximize your oxygen intake. This will give your body a head start, since cold showers cause one to breath deeply as your body requires additional oxygen to keep warm. There is no getting around the breathing reflex experienced when entering a cold shower, but doing a breathing exercise prior to entering the shower with help your body acclimate more smoothly. Breath deeply into your lungs and exhale gently when doing the exercise. Once you have completed the deep breathing, get yourself pumped up and excited about the amazing benefits you are about to obtain from getting in the cold water. Thinking about the cold shower experience this way will make it a lot more enjoyable for you. Turn your shower on to cold and jump in. I like to get right under the shower head initially so water finds its way to most of my body. You don't want to have cold water running on your scalp the whole time though, since this can cause a brain freeze or headache- especially as a beginner. To counter this, I recommend that you stand back a few inches and aim the water for your chest area. Wash your hair, body, whatever you need to do. When you are rinsing in the shower, rub your arms, chest, and legs to help warm yourself up. Observe your body once you've been in the shower for over 2 or 3 minutes. Your skin will be flushed red from the circulatory changes you are experiencing. I like to aim for a 3-5 minute ice cold shower, but once you've passed the 3 minute mark, you are done.

The Post Cold Shower Experience

Get out of the shower and begin drying off. How do you feel? You should feel cold on the outside, but notice how your body is starting to warm up as it works to increase its internal temperature naturally. Notice the change in your skin tone upon exiting the shower. It is amazing how exposure to the cold water changes your circulatory systems behaviour, and the evidence of this is observable on your skin. Those who don't expose themselves to cold conditions via cold showers simply don't experience these physical benefits. Unfortunately, without practicing cold therapy via cold showers, their body is not activated and used to the fullest very often. Cold showers allow us to unlock the full use of our circulatory system, and this is one of their most powerful physical benefits.

CHAPTER THREE

Why Cold Shower?

Perhaps you the reader are wondering, why should I cold shower? So far I've outlined how I started cold showering, and how to take your first cold shower, and the immediate experience as you exit the shower- but I haven't told you WHY you need to cold shower in general. There are a ton of reasons why you should cold shower. Personally, I've noticed over the last two years of taking cold showers a number of unique benefits. Let's start with the physical recovery benefits.

Physical Recovery Benefits

Muscle Recovery

I live a fairly active lifestyle. I workout in the gym about 4 times a week doing powerlifting and general weight training. When I'm not in the gym, I'm boxing with friends or hiking in the outdoors of beautiful British Columbia, Canada. All this activity puts stress on my muscles and joints. I've noticed that when I have a ice cold shower after my training sessions or hikes, my recovery is improved. In particular, I experience a great reduction in muscle inflammation and soreness from my cold showers. After highly intensive training where ones muscles are pushed to their limits, delayed onset muscle soreness or DOMS can set in. I'm sure you've experienced this after a big workout or perhaps a hard tennis match. The next day you wake up with aching muscles, and it might even make getting out of bed a struggle. This is DOMS. Delayed onset muscle soreness occurs as a result of the microscopic tears and inflammation of the muscle fibres that happens during exercise. Cold showers have been studied and shown to help counter the symptoms of muscle tearing and inflammation. Cold water lowers the temperature of tissue fibre and constricts blood vessels, leading to a reduction in swelling and inflammation. It has also been suggested that cold exposure can numb nerve endings, leading to pain relief. It isn't surprising then why so many athletes take part in cold showers and other cold therapy (e.g. cryotherapy, ice baths) after workouts. However, the physical recovery benefits of cold showers are not exclusive to athletes and the active.

Like many people in the 21st century, I'm very inactive at times. For instance, I spend a lot of time sitting in front of a computer when I'm working on my businesses. Being bound to a chair has lead to me experiencing many aches and pains in my lower back. If you work in an office settings or sit behind a computer at your work, I'm sure you can relate to this. In the past I tried to limit the amount of time I stayed seated, and I've done extensive research on stretches to alleviate lower back pain online-but nothing has worked that well. That was until I tried cold showers. Cold showers have definitely helped with my back pain. It has not eliminated it completely, I still experience back pain at times, but it does help alleviate it for me.

Fat Loss

Many cold shower enthusiasts rave about their fat loss benefits. I myself have always been a fairly lean guy, but even I noticed with regular cold showers that my body was getting more toned. However, people with excess weight are able to take advantage of the full fat-burning effects of cold showers. In fact, a close friend of mine was able to lose over 50lbs of fat over a period of one year using a cold shower and intermittent fasting protocol. So how do cold showers cause fat loss? It has to do with something called brown fat. Cold temperatures have been shown in many scientific studies to increase the activation of brown fat in the body. Brown fat (aka brown adipose tissue) is our special 'energy-burning' body fat that produces heat and burns significant amounts of calories to help maintain our body's core temperature in cold conditions. A Harvard study by Lans et al., found that people who spent 10 consecutive days in cooled rooms increased their brown fat levels significantly. The more brown fat you have, the more calories you should be able to burn in theory when exposed to cold. Also, one study in the New England Journal of Medicine by Cypress et al., found that the amount of brown fat in humans is inversely correlated with body mass. So definitely take cold showers to activate your brown fat, increase your brown fat, and finally burn excess calories with your 'energy-burning' brown fat. Also just so you know- most adults carry the majority of their brown fat around their neck and shoulders, so you should have no problem getting it activated in the cold shower.

Improved Immunity

In a Netherlands study, Buijze et al. found that people who ended their showers with cold water for at least 30 seconds for one month called in sick 29% less than the group that engaged in regular warm showers. Short periods of cold stress like what you will get from a 2 to 5 minute cold shower are a highly effective way to improve the immune system. Scientists have found that cold stress for up to 2 hours has been shown to boost immune function. Of course you will likely not expose yourself to the cold for 2 hours in a single session, but it is likely that even short daily exposures can help boost your immune function, especially over time. Studies conducted by Delahanty et al., and Brenner et al., found that general and local cold water exposure demonstrated an increase in NK count and activity in humans. NK cells or Natural killer cells are critical to the innate immune system. Natural killer cells respond to virus-infected cells in the body and also respond to tumor formation. It is amazing how cold showers can be used to boost NK cell production in our body naturally, and the method (taking a cold shower) is efficient and easy to implement compared to taking costly drugs or supplements. Studies by Brenner et al., also found that the decrease in body temperature from cold water exposure led to a statistically significant elevation in circulating Interleukin 6 (IL-6) concentrations. Interleukin 6 is a protein that helps regulate immune responses. IL-6 also helps in the maintenance and health of astrocytes, which are cells in the human brain. During the human body's immune response, IL-6 is secreted by white blood cells. Low concentrations of IL-6 have been linked to cancer and arthritis in humans. So if cold showers have the potential to naturally increase levels of this beneficial protein in my body, I can't complain.

Circulatory System Stimulation

As the body attempts to warm itself up, this causes your heart to pump blood more rapidly. This improves circulation and overall cardiac function, as the heart muscles need to work hard to pump blood to the periphery of your body to warm it. Moving blood to the periphery of the body also supports cognitive function, since blood to the brain is increased. By taking cold showers, you allow your body to function at a higher level and do what it is meant to do. Someone who doesn't expose themselves to cold showers may not get the same blood pumping effects to the periphery of their body, or their brain. It's akin to not using the full capacity of a cars technology or engine. If driven seldomly and rarely used, parts and technology in the car will stop performing well, and over time may fail altogether. This is why it is so important to engage your body and brain to the fullest degree. In the distant past, our ancestors body's would have been used to the fullest due to their harsh living conditions. Why wouldn't you want to unlock and use your body the way it was meant to be like our ancestors did?

Improves Hair & Skin

Improvements to ones hair and skin is another great benefit of cold showers that is often overlooked by cold therapy enthusiasts. Many individuals often look to cold showers for fat loss or muscle recovery benefits and don't realize that this amazing activity can also do wonders for your skin and hair. One way cold showers improve your skin and hair is by constricting the blood vessels close to your skins surface. The constriction of blood flow can give ones skin and hair a healthier look. Hot water showers on the other hand strip the surface of our skin and hair of essential oils, leaving our skin dry, and our hair brittle. This symptom of hot showers is especially awful if you have pre-existing dry skin/hair, eczema, or acne. I suffered from dry skin on the face and hands in the past, and my habit of taking cold showers has got rid of these symptoms completely. My skin feels much more soft and hydrated on a daily basis since opting out of hot showers.

As you can now see, there are a ton of physical benefits cold showers can yield. Whether you want to improve the quality of your skin, tone your muscles, or improve your immune system, a cold shower is a remedy to consider. Now I'm going to discuss some of the psychological benefits of cold showers.

Mental Benefits

A Potential Anti-Depressant

Cold showers may be a potential treatment for depression. Depression is a term used to describe a wide range of depressive mood disorders. These depressive disorders include bipolar, depression, and dysthymia to name a few. Depression is a common mental health disability, with approximately 10% of the adult population of the USA suffering from some form of the illness. Perhaps you or someone you know is suffering from this all too common disorder. I know many people in my circle that have suffered or are suffering from some form of depression. One thing I hear often from some of my friends is that they either aren't enthusiastic about taking prescribed pharmaceutical medication, or they don't enjoy how the medication makes them feel. Many depression sufferers also say that their medication alleviated symptoms of depression but lead to other unwanted side effects like weight gain or decreased libido. While I do not have the authority to tell someone to avoid or stop taking medication, I will say that being able to implement a natural remedy like cold showers to aid in your treatment of a depressive disorder is a powerful thing, and perhaps it is something you can add in your life in addition to your other treatments for depression. If you are depressed, why not make cold showers part of your daily routine. One theory for cold showers as a treatment for depression compares the shock of the cold water to a gentle electroconvulsive therapy. **Electroconvulsive therapy** (ECT), is a medical treatment in which seizures are electrically induced in patients to provide relief from mental disorders. The cold water hitting your body during a shower may send electrical impulses to the nerve endings of the brain and therefore increase ones alertness and energy levels. Feel good hormones called endorphins are also released during cold showers. The endorphin release will also increase feelings of happiness and well-being.

Improved Energy & Focus

Improved energy and focus is definitely one of my favourite benefits of cold showers. When you get in the cold water, you are immediately given a jolt of energy and your mind and body wakes up. A cold shower in the morning is really akin to a morning cup of coffee. If you are a coffee drinker, I suggest you try starting your morning with a cold shower. See how you feel before you have your coffee. I think you will find that without your caffeine, you are perfectly energized and awake. I still like to enjoy my coffee, don't get me wrong, but I seriously think cold showers could be a potential natural replacement for one's morning caffeine. The improved energy and focus you get from cold showers is remarkable as well because it isn't just a short term benefit. The energizing effect lasts throughout the day. The reason why cold showers yield this amazing benefit is due to something called norepinephrine. Norepinephrine is a chemical that functions in the human brain and body as a hormone. Norepinephrine is used to call the brain and body to action. So it's levels are lowest during sleep and calm states. Levels of norepinephrine rise during times of stress. For example, levels rise significantly during a flight-or-fight response and increase energy and alertness. Researchers have concluded that cold showers can create a similar response in the body and increase norepinephrine release by over 200 percent with a basic protocol. Just a few cold showers per week can increase norepinephrine release significantly.

CHAPTER FOUR

Challenging Yourself with the Colder Shower Ritual

Although all the physical and psychological benefits of cold showers I've reviewed are amazing, I don't consider any of them to be the most important reason to take a plunge into the cold. Ultimately, the greatest single reason to take cold showers is because it is a worthwhile challenge. What you get on the other side, after sacrificing your warmth and comfort, is ultimate bliss. If you take it further and make the cold shower a daily or weekly ritually, you will benefit even further from it. Culture today is all about making things easier and more comfortable. Heating in homes, food delivery, and warm showers all make our lives more comfy. All this comfort people experience leads to a desensitizing of feeling. Human beings are largely never pushing their own limits of sensation and experience. We avoid discomfort, stress, or challenging situations like the plague. However, when you decide to challenge your mind and body with an activity like a frigid cold shower, you will find that in the discomfort of the cold shower there is an incredible feeling of vitality. This is what I want you the reader to understand. The weight loss benefits, the improvement of skin quality to name a few are all amazing things, but these are simply additional benefits. The overall vibrancy you experience from leaving your warm bed every morning and challenging yourself with a cold shower is what you should be after. It may be tough, you may not want to get in the cold water, but I assure you once you do you will set an amazing tone for the whole day. By taking cold showers, you will also build up an incredible resilience to stressors in your daily life. Since you've conditioned your mind and body to accept and deal with stress in a controlled environment (the cold shower), you will be much better prepared for real pressure and stress that is commonly faced whether at work, home, or school. Next thing you know, you will want to make cold showers a part of your life routine, whether it is daily or weekly. I know from experience, since I've made cold showers part of both my morning and night ritual. Of course, I've had the odd warm shower in the last two years, but I make sure I expose myself to cold showers at least 5 times a week to this day.

CHAPTER FIVE

Building Your Cold Shower Routine

You can go a few ways with regards to ritualizing or routinizing your cold shower. Some people opt for a daily split routine. In that case, the cold shower practitioner gets one cold shower in per day, but may have one regular shower as well. For example, one may have a 5 minute morning cold shower, but every evening have a regular shower. Personally, I try to go cold every time I shower, and I only take warm showers when it feels absolutely necessary, but the split routine is more suitable for some people. If you feel like strictly cold showering isn't for you- then maybe you should consider a daily split. Another way you can approach your cold shower is with a weekday/weekend split routine. This is a very interesting way to build a habit for your cold shwoers, and it is a great approach for people who like to set goals. The name says it all. A weekday/weekend split routine is when you could shower Monday to Friday, but have a warm shower on the weekends. There are 3 main reasons this can make for an awesome cold shower ritual. For one, having your cold showers on the weekdays provides you with all the awesome benefits during your work week (assuming you work Monday to Friday). Second, by exposing yourself to only cold water for 5 days straight, you will experience more of the fat burning benefits of the cold shower. The more time you expose yourself to cold water, the more brown fat in your body you will activate, so this routine is perfect for those who are focused on fat loss. The third reason I love this ritual is because you have something to look forward to on the weekends. After challenging yourself with cold showers all week, you will feel amazing being in warm water on the weekends. Don't get me wrong- cold showers are amazing and after having them you feel great, but the act of having them is always a challenge. They get easier, but there is always discomfort, so warm water is a great treat after having nothing but cold showers for a week straight! The last way to ritualize your cold showers is to become a cold shower "lifer" with the lifer routine. The lifer routine for cold showers is when you simply cold shower every day, and only deviate from the routine if absolutely necessary. This is a routine for the hardcore only. By being a cold shower lifer, you give your mind and body the greatest chance to reap the full benefits of this practice. When you cold shower only a few times a week, you can still get a lot of benefits in the areas of mood, circulation, and fat loss, but you lose out slightly on other benefits like improvements in skin and hair. At least, that's what I've noticed in my experience so far. The few times I've veered away from my routine, I've noticed things like dry skin coming up. Of course, everything is different, and your skin may be perfectly fine from hot water exposure. But to avoid this, keep your routine consistent and stick with it suing either a weekday/weekend or lifer routine. You will experience massive results, and over time your cold shower ritual will be second nature.

CHAPTER SIX

So far this book has provided you with information on how to cold shower, the benefits and science of cold showers, and routines to follow when embarking on this journey. I am now going to discuss a few facts about cold showers that will help you stay on course. Whether you are someone who has cold showered before, or a complete beginner, there will be moments where you don't want to continue cold showering. Perhaps you may even turn the water to warm midway through your first cold shower. Cold showers are not an easy thing and you must be ready to feel discomfort. So to stay on course during this journey, always remember why you chose to try cold showers in the first place. Perhaps you wanted to lose some weight, improve the quality of your skin, or alleviate symptoms of depression. Cold showers have the ability to help with all those aforementioned things, so when you are feeling extreme discomfort under the cold water, recall that. Remember that if you stick with your cold shower routine, you will experience incredible results. When you are struggling to motivate yourself to get into the cold water, remember that these showers are essentially a form of resilience training. The average person in western society today is avoiding discomfort and stress at all costs. Separate yourself from the ordinary and accept the challenge of cold showers. The stress you have to deal with in your cold shower will prepare your mind and body for real stress that you may face in your daily life, and that's a powerful thing.

By now you should know about the vast benefits of cold showers, how to cold shower, how to create a cold shower routine, and lastly how to stay on course with cold showers. I hope you enjoyed reading my book. Please consider giving my book a review, it would be much appreciated.

Printed in Great Britain
by Amazon